DISCARD

Dirty Signs

**The World's 150 Most
Unfortunately Named
Streets, Towns and Places**

Rob Bailey and Ed Hurst

Ulysses Press

Published in the U.S. by
Ulysses Press
P.O. Box 3440
Berkeley, CA 94703
www.ulyssespress.com

First published in the U.K. as **Rude World** (2006) and **Rude UK** (2007) by Boxtree, an imprint of Pan Macmillan Ltd.

ISBN: 978-1-56975-554-9
Library of Congress Control Number 2008911724

Design: what!design @ whatweb.com
Editorial and Production: Claire Chun, Nick Denton-Brown, Bryce Willett, Abby Reser, Elyce Petker

Printed in Korea by Tara TPS through Four Colour Print Group

10 9 8 7 6 5 4 3 2 1

This book has been made possible by generous submissions and assistance from a wide range of people across the world. All images are individually credited apart from those places photographed personally by the authors.

Distributed by Publishers Group West

INTRODUCTION

Welcome to **Dirty Signs**! Within these pages are all of the completely-inappropriate-yet-real signs you saw and wanted to snap photos of but didn't. Or maybe you were just too oblivious to decipher anything dirty about them. Well...those days are over.

Snickering at "Weener" aside, these signs represent more than a preteen sense of humor. We inhabit an increasingly interconnected planet in which people thousands of miles apart can communicate instantaneously. This kind of communication, and the technology (like cell phones, internet chat rooms and Facebook) that supports it, has created a new, perverse form of abbreviated English. It is this new language that is slipping its way into different societies around the world.

Because of this global melting pot of cultures, some fear we are entering an age in which we all speak and think in the same way. Others believe that the opposite is occurring: cultures are adopting intolerant, antagonistic positions to ensure that they survive the move toward globalization.

Set against this conflict, why are Shitterton, Middlefart and Kunst-Wet so important?

Dirty-sounding names are powerful because they represent a microcosm of the challenges facing the planet. They inspire shared merriment, bring people together and foster understanding as people explore one another's languages and histories. Although the things people find funny vary immensely, humor it-self is profoundly human. No piece of technology can replace two people sharing a joke. To learn a language is go beyond "LOL" and e-mail and to actually talk to people. That is how you learn about a culture and sometimes even pick up a few dirty words or phrases. Who knows? You might even return home, see a sign and realize it means "vagina" in Portuguese.

It is our belief that, as we snicker at these dirty-sounding names and share our amusement with those who do not understand, we can come together and learn more about our common humanity and the power of language. Mutual respect and open-mindedness are as vital now as they have ever been, from global geopolitics to every-day human life. By joining **Dirty Signs**' journey through our planet's place names, we can all play a part in achieving greater harmony. In these times of global tension and misunderstanding, the opportunity to foster respect and warmth by revealing dirty interpretations of innocent signs, town names and train stations cannot be missed.

You are now on a brave journey through a kaleidoscope of place names, cultures and languages. Join us on this adventure and together let us share global under-standing and respect as we play a vital part in developing a world that is at once joined together and boundlessly varied.

If you would like to take part in the ongoing quest to gather and understand dirty place and street names, please visit us at www.rude-world.co.uk.

Rob Bailey and Ed Hurst
April 2009

DIRTY SIGNS

EXIT 4C

94 NORTH

Blairstown

½ MILE

EXIT 4B

46 EAST

Portland PA

Buttzville

¼ MILE

Home of the anus sandwich.
Buttzville, New Jersey

Where Monica Lewinsky got her start in politics.
Climax, Minnesota

If there's grass on the field, play ball.
County Donegal, Ireland

GOLDEN BALLS ROUNDABOUT

Stadhampton B 4015 (B 480)

Oxford
A 4074

Reading
Wallingford
A 4074

Henley (A 4130)

Once you sleep with 1,000 women, you can dip 'em in gold and have them immortalized.
Oxfordshire, UK

That's the way he likes it.
Northwood, Middlesex, UK

What else you gonna do in a town like this?
Bavaria, Germany

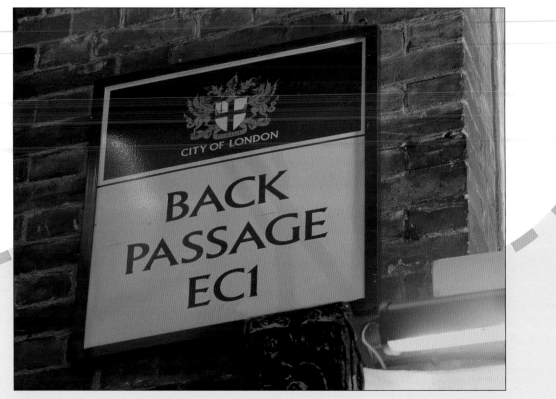

Be sure to lube up before going down this alley.
London, UK

Time to do some squats.
Heptonstall, West Yorkshire, UK

Where the congregation gets down on its knees to pray.
Beaverlick, Kentucky

Three kilometers is a long way to walk just for a little weener.
Lower Saxony, Germany

The little bump before you get to heaven.
Dornoch, Sutherland, UK

So what's there to do around here?
Fucking, Austria

Hopefully it leads to a dead end.
Fallon, Nevada

Photo: Jim Dowling

...and I'll show you.
Prague, Czech Republic

Caution: This path leads to violent spasms and shrieks of ecstasy.
Leeds, West Yorkshire, UK

...and around the corners.
Brentford, Middlesex, UK

Fun for the whole family.
Boone, Kentucky

And you wonder why small town people are so bitter.
Waldviert, Austria

Ready, aim...
Martinborough, New Zealand

Sounds like these guys could use a little more experience.
Pilling, Lancashire, UK

Sometimes any hole will do.
Devon, UK

Where you can go, but never come.
Hull, Humberside, UK

Warm milk served daily.
Brittany, France

A sign from the oral sex gods.
Dalgety Bay, Fife, UK

Wan King Path

28·14 灣景街

By the end of the day, it gets a little slippery.
Sai Kung, Hong Kong

Photo: Tom Mangan, 2005

If you let your bum get passed, you'll be in hell.
Lassen Volcanic National Park, California

Make sure it's clean before you go in there.
Penryn, Cornwall, UK

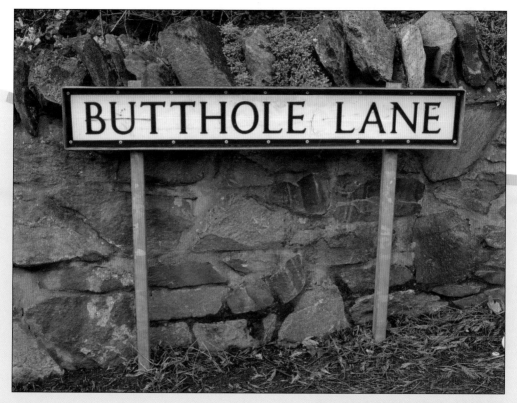

The backdoor way to heaven.
Shepshed, Leicestershire, UK

He likes to go long.
Hampton, Middlesex, UK

Jane Austen's pet names for her favorite orifice.
Swansea, Wales (left) and London, UK (right)

Beware of sudden gusts.
St. Andrews, Scotland

FURRY WAY

Sounds like somebody needs to trim.
Helston, Cornwall, UK

Just say no to bastards.
Umbria, Italy

No morons allowed.
Andalucia, Spain

Obviously, you need a condom if you're going to "lectoure" your girl's passage.
Gers, France

Many a man has called this place home.
Besthorpe, Norfolk, UK

Crap Sés
700 m

"...he who goes to bed with itchy butthole wakes up with stinky finger."
Graubünden, Switzerland

Go together like horse and carriage.
New York, NY

How's Studley Roger supposed to be studly if he has to drive carefully?
North Yorkshire, UK

You should cut off before you reach this point.
Iowa City, Iowa

Photo: Kim Jordan

It's wide open and ready to be parked in.
Lower Froyle, Hampshire, UK

PILBARA IRON

← PARKER POINT
EAST INTERCOURSE ISLAND →

OVERLENGTH VEHICLE CROSSING

The sun's not the only thing that rises in the East.
East Intercourse, Australia

It doesn't have to be bald, I just don't want a jungle down there.
London, UK

The best way to warm up your fingers on a cold winter's night.
Essex, UK

She must be hot to have landed a saint.
Cornwall, UK

Must be impressive to get its own listing.
Isle of Arran, Scotland

For those who like it rough.
Burbage, Wiltshire, UK

FONDAMENTA
DE CA LABIA

The local mechanic is Labia Grease Monkeys.
Venice, Italy

Oh, so if a street has lots of residents, it's called a hoe. But if a town has lots, that's considered normal. What a double standard.

Watford, Hertfordshire, UK

French kissing for people without lips.
French Lick, Indiana

Where the world's hormones go for release.
Nyon, Switzerland

40s and hookers. It's Snoop Dogg's paradise.
Westminster, Colorado

THE GREEN
LEADING TO
STICKY LANE

Drive carefully and be sure to strap up for protection.
Hardwicke Greene, Gloucestershire, UK

Me so horni.
Prague, Czech Republic

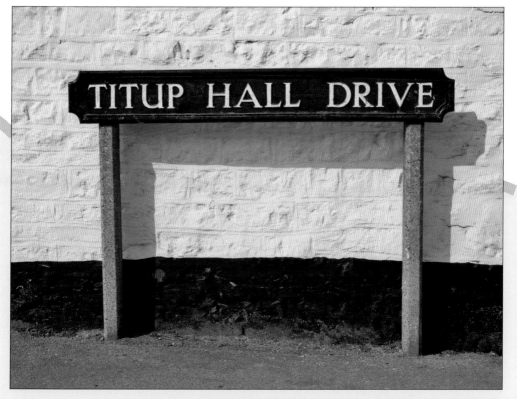

Don't get down on yourself. Keep your tit up.
Headington, Oxfordshire, UK

Prehistoric dildos.
South Yorkshire, UK

SEAMONS CLOSE

Of course it is. It's a constantly renewable resource.
Dunstable, Bedfordshire, UK

Good work, fellas. Only took seven of you to get it done.
Brussels, Belgium

That's the one where you tuck it under your waistband and hope nobody notices.
London, UK

Breathe through your mouth.
Windpassing, Austria

Every plumber's dream home.
Cornwall, UK

Every man should know his way around these parts.
Celles, Belgium

Nasty don't roll like that.
Hertfordshire, UK

We're soooo going to hell for this.
Oxford, UK

Holy erection!
London, UK

Of course they do. They've got needs just like the rest of us.
Kent, UK

Horrible place to be from, but at least it's a conversation starter.
Bere Regis, Dorset, UK

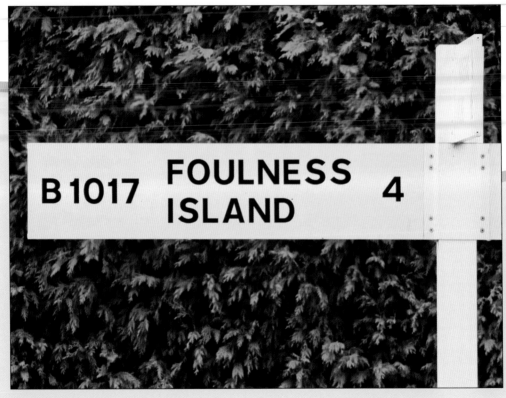

It's like a crappy Club Med.
Essex, UK

Go through the end of Dicken...
St. Gallen, Switzerland

...and you'll shoot out right into Cunter.
Graubünden, Switzerland

Manbreasts can be beautiful too.
Somerton, Somerset, UK

Home of the annual Wife Swap Meet.
Ashover, Derbyshire, UK

Watch for flying debris.
Headington, Oxfordshire, UK

Photo: Nanette and Dan Wells

Is the speed limit really necessary? Do you honestly think any guy is going to drive that fast while getting his knob licked?
Knob Lick, Missouri

It feels so good.
Lancaster, UK

Gynecology capital of the world.
Lincolnshire, UK

Stay stronger, longer on Hardon Road.
Wolverhampton, West Midlands, UK

Welcome To
MEAT COVE
THE MOST
NORTHERN
COMMUNITY
1 – MEAT COVE MOUNTAIN TRAIL
2 – RIVER TRAIL
3 – FRASER TRAIL
4 – GRASSY POINT TRAIL
5 – CAPE ST. LAWRENCE TRAIL

Photo: Shannon Burt, www.trailpeak.com

Follow the grassy trail to Meat Cove.
Nova Scotia, Canada

The campsite's a dump.
Cantabria, Spain

Hmmm, a deserted field in the middle of nowhere called Sodom Lane. I wonder what happens here.

Dauntsey, Wiltshire, UK

Oh does he now?
Oxfordshire, UK

Photo: Hans Splinter, www.flickr.com/photos/archeon

Where hobbits go to blow ass.
Funen, Denmark

That's it? I think I'd rather take my chances on Cockhell.
Bishopsteignton, Devon, UK

MT MEE
TOURIST DRIVE
LENGTH 40 km
FOLLOW

TOURIST DRIVE
29

The mountain was asking for it, officer.
Queensland, Australia

Technically it arcs, but who's counting?
Wailuku River State Park, Hilo, Hawaii

Big cocks coming through.
Hoddesdon, Hertfordshire, UK

Someone must put a stop to this anti-wang campaign!
Wieselburger Land, Austria

Now with more scrotum flavor.
Valencia, Spain

You got two of 'em and we wanna see 'em.
Tidikelt, Algeria

It smells like what they swallow. I mean, eat.
Schiltberg, Germany

Petting
Kreis Traunstein

COME BY CHANCE

Photo: Neil Smith, Fort St. John, BC

It's a Puritan town, but as long as you keep it above the clothes, it's all good.
Bavaria, Germany

Not since I was 12.
Newfoundland, Canada

It's just like Disneyland...for 25-year-old guys with big-titted mermaid fetishes.
Lower Saxony, Germany

It's the largest town around, so locals call it Big Titty Ho.
Raunds, Northamptonshire, UK

Young, sexy "Bonnie and Clyde" Faye or old, cougarish "Rules of Attraction" Faye?
Guildford, Surrey, UK

Stop?! But I've already breached the hole!
Oahu, Hawaii

Photo: Jamie Deeman

Happens to the best of us.
South Island, New Zealand

Did somebody call a farmer? Bow-chicka-bow-wow.
Ingolstadt, Germany

I like to get a nice stropping when I'm horny too.
Chko, Czech Republic

Make him sleep on it.
County Durham, UK

Get your dick pierced where it all started.
Western Cape, South Africa

Life on Dick Lane is pretty, um, hard.
Bradford, West Yorkshire, UK

All right, I'll rim her, but she'd better return the favor.
Huyton, Merseyside, UK

EXIT 69

Big Beaver Rd

Big rigs coming through.
Big Beaver, Michigan

Don't let the name fool you, the town is actually shit.
Pukë, Albania

Even clergy isn't immune to crabs.
Warwickshire, UK

Hmmm...tough choice.
Savoie, France

Horse rape. It's no joke.
Norfolk, UK

Makeout Point was so 1990s.
South Island, New Zealand

Spiritual home to 12-year-old boys all over the world.
North Rhine-Westphalia, Germany

If the wool crop is weak, they add a little of this to fluff things out.
London, UK

Stick it in the wrong crescent and you'll end up with a nasty case of dickburn.
Bonnyridge, Stirlingshire, UK

Shafter? I barely know her!
Shafter, California

What a perv.
North Rhine-Westphalia, Germany

**On this line, everybody rides
for free.**
Ekerö, Sweden

Only go down this road as a last resort.
Cambuslang, Scotland

FROGGATT EDGE 8 M

SHATTON MOOR 3½ M.

BROUGH 2½ M.

How much more could they have been shat on?
Derbyshire, UK

The dick always points to the triangle.
Kingston upon Thames, Surrey, UK

Keep it trimmed, baby. It's like a safari every time we sleep together.
Scoulton, Norfolk, UK

If you swallow, I'll drive however you want.
Lincolnshire, UK

Directions to the most well-hung leprechaun ever.
Berkshire, UK

Aren't bikes with seats supposed to protect you from Rimsting?
Bavaria, Germany

Eat up.
Punxsutawney, Pennsylvania

Photo: Camilla Rivera (Cami)

I do. I rue the bitch every damn day.
Strasbourg, France

The panoramas are breathtaking.
Chester Le Street, County Durham, UK

Fresh flesh here. Get your flesh.
Edinburgh, UK

15 miles?!? I'll give you 12 and that's my final offer.
Tightwad, Missouri

Don't give up. You're so close to your goal.
Albrighton, Shropshire, UK

Töss

11 Hauptbahnhof

...my salad.
Zürich, Switzerland

Typical aliens. They shag you once and never call again.
Nova Scotia, Canada

Do you really need directions?
Schwyz, Switzerland

Way more hazardous than Golden Shower Way.
Florham Park, New Jersey

Larry Craig's favorite water closet.
North Rhine-Westphalia, Germany

Photo: Ed Lee

It's like the Silk Road, but better.
Kowloon, Hong Kong

Open to the whole neighborhood.
Leighton Buzzard, Bedfordshire, UK

Like I need you to tell me when to do this, sign. You're just a stupid, inanimate object.
Brussels, Belgium

It's a nicer version of hell, so the sign's only half burnt.
North Yorkshire, UK

It finally happened.
Hell, Michigan

It may be the world's oldest profession, but an entire industry?
Bütschwil, Switzerland

This way for booty floss.
Kent, UK

They're big in Dicker, but you should see how well-hung they are in Horsebridge.
East Sussex, UK

Your mother-in-law after too much chili con carne.
Waidhofen, Austria

Just follow your nose.
Stinking Creek, Tennessee

Shouldn't the arrow be pointing down?
Newfoundland, Canada

Photo: Mike Haber

You're damn right it's private. I'm making a peepee.
Hana, Maui, Hawaii

Photo: Steve Alpert

All roads lead to Mianus.
Mianus, Connecticut

Photo: Rachel Morgan-Trimmer, www.thecareerbreaksite.com

Every man's favorite port to dock in.
Moissac, France

ABOUT THE AUTHORS

Rob Bailey spent his formative years in the village of Cumnor, Oxfordshire. His family's home rested peacefully upon the hill known as Tumbledown Dick. He lives in Oxford with a small family of guitars.

Ed Hurst, in common with Isaac Newton, was born in the Lincolnshire town of Grantham. His blend of pompous and puerile verbosity has helped him to establish himself as a management consultant. Ed is proud of the fact that he knows how to pronounce "Glenmorangie."